GOLDEN NUGGETS FROM A LIFE WELL LIVED

BY MELODY C. THOMAS

For more information:
249 Rainbow Dr, Box 14923, Livingston, TX 77399

Library of Congress Cataloging-in-Publication Data is available.

ISBN 979-8-9858351-0-6 (HC)
ISBN 979-8-9858351-1-3 (PB)
ISBN 979-8-9858351-2-0 (E)

BIAC Categories: Life Experience, Humor, Education
SEL-021000 Motivational & Inspirational
BIO-026000 Personal Memoirs
EDU-029110 Teaching/Subjects/General

Cover design by KUHN Design Group | kuhndesigngroup.com

PRINTED IN THE UNITED STATES OF AMERICA

Dedication

Dedicated to Stanley R. Brett, PhD who helped me learn to
love myself and, ultimately, the world around me.
You saved me and I am forever grateful. Thank you.

Foreword

I was talking with my daughter one day when she mentioned that something I said to her as a teenager made her feel empowered: "You always have a choice. You might not like the choices you have, but you always have a choice." I then remembered that my son had often repeated another of my sayings: "Things could always be worse."

Suddenly, it seemed that many of the things I had said over the years were inspirational or educational. I taught college, gave sermons at my church, served as a commander and inspector general in the US Army, led scout troops, assumed leadership positions in various organizations, and imparted ideas and advice to many people over the years. I have learned a lot during my time on this earth. Much of it is worth sharing in the hope that others can benefit from my experience.

In this book, I have listed many of the sayings and beliefs I have picked up over the years. Some I have discussed in detail. Others I have simply listed for you to interpret and ponder as you will. In my career as an educator, I enjoyed sharing my experience with students. My greatest joy was seeing a student's eyes light up with sudden understanding. I hope this book will also help to guide and educate you on your own life journey. May your eyes light with understanding.

My Background

I was the oldest of five children born to a US Air Force sergeant and housewife. I had a half-brother (from my father's first marriage), three brothers, and one sister. We moved around, as any Air Force family does, until we landed in Virginia and my parents split up. I was twelve; the youngest was less than a year old.

My mother was the child of Russian immigrants. She dropped out of school in the tenth grade and went to work as a nurse's aide in the former Central Islip Psychiatric Hospital on Long Island in New York, living in a small room on the property. That's where she met my father (he was visiting friends). She was twenty-one (considered a spinster at that time); he was thirty. All the girls got married right out of high school and had two or three kids by the time they were in their twenties. I don't know if she ever really "loved" him but my mother accepted his marriage proposal. They got married and nine months, two weeks later, I arrived. My father was stationed at Maguire Air Force Base in New Jersey and I was born in the Army hospital next door at Fort Dix.

We then drove across country to California where my mother, my nine-year-old half-brother, and I lived for a year before we could join my father in Okinawa. After a year overseas, we returned to the United States by ship and drove back across country to New York where my father served five years at Mitchell Air Force Base on Long Island (the base has since become a community college). Two brothers and a sister were born in Hempstead before my father was transferred to the Netherlands for a three-year tour of duty. Normally, the Air Force required service members to wait one year before their family could join them (that's why we stayed in California for a year). I guess that was to ensure they could establish a suitable household. My grandfather, who had been born in Holland, went ahead to secure a house for us to live in. My father claimed he was going to live with relatives and was allowed to bring us with him when he first reported for duty. Grandpa lived with us for a short time before returning to the United States.

While my father had a drinking problem, it got increasingly worse during our three years in Holland.

My youngest brother was born in June 1962, and we returned to the United States in October of that year. My father was assigned to Andrews Air Force Base and we lived in Virginia. Soon after returning to the US, my parents had a fight one night, and my father was hitting my mother. I got out of bed and ran to put myself between them. The next day, my mother threw him out. There was my father, kneeling on the porch, crying, and begging us to ask Mommy to let him stay. We cried and screamed, begging my mother to let Daddy stay, but she was like a stone, unmoved by our pleas for mercy. I felt so powerless and unable to affect anything. This was a life changing moment for me. I swore I would never be helpless again.

Let me add that my mother came from an alcoholic family. Her parents emigrated from Russia in 1912. They had eight children. My mother was number seven, born in 1929, the year of the Wall Street stock market crash that prefaced the Great Depression. Her parents were uneducated and worked odd jobs–grandpa as a janitor, grandma as a scrubwoman (as my mother described her). During prohibition, they made liquor (hooch) in the bathtub. I guess that's how they both became alcoholics. My mother recounted stories of ferocious fights between her parents with verbal as well as physical bouts. One night, her mother staggered into the hallway with a hatchet stuck between her eyes. The three youngest children (my mother and two sisters) were put in an orphanage when things got bad, then reclaimed when things got better. My uncle once told me they were thrown out of their apartment every year for nonpayment of rent. I can understand why my mother left at age sixteen. She never saw her mother again. It was a violent upbringing and one my mother did not want for her children. Grandma died of cancer when I was just a year old. I never met her.

The ensuing years after my parents split were rough. My mother's sister Jean and her three children came to live with us in Newport News, Virginia. I was the oldest and left to watch everyone (eight of us) while my mother and aunt worked. They were both waitresses. In addition, my mother drove a Mister Softee ice cream truck and taught classes at Arthur Murray dance studios. Still, we did not have enough to eat. We wore no shoes during the summer in order to save them for school. We took a piece of bread smeared with lard and sprinkled with sugar for lunch and sipped water from the fountain at school. It was oatmeal for breakfast and spaghetti for dinner–when there was food in the house.

Our house was in a poor, run-down neighborhood inhabited mostly by blacks, and we were called the "po' white trash down the street." This was during the 1960s, and civil-rights riots were happening all over the place. We constantly got into fights with the other kids in the neighborhood. After my one-year-old brother was hurt in one of our clashes, my mother sent him to live with another sister, Anne, in New York.

A fire in the chimney burned a hole in the exterior side of the second floor. I remember the seven of us crawling between the mattress and box spring to cuddle together for warmth and watching snow come through the hole to gently gather on top of the mattress.

About a year after moving in together, my mother and her sister had a big fight. My aunt took her three kids and left. We moved to a large farmhouse in the country in Mattaponi, about an hour outside of Newport News. A woman with her two girls came to stay at the house. She was mean, always pulling her children's hair and calling them names. We didn't like her very much. My brother and I came across a snake in the field one day, killed it, and put it in the woman's bed. I think you could hear the scream all the way back to the city. It was very satisfying and well worth the punishment we suffered. My mother stayed in Newport News during the week and came out to the farm on weekends. We lived there over the summer.

When the semester started, there was no room in the local school for two of us, so we moved back to New York and stayed with my mother's sister Anne for a little while. Anne's husband and infant child had died, leaving her with six children to care for (Anne had also taken in my youngest brother after our shenanigans in Newport News). She took in ironing for a living and the place always smelled like starch and had clothes hanging everywhere. It was crowded with eleven kids running around. We complained and demanded to go live with our father. He had not kept in touch with us and I don't think we had seen or heard from him in over three years, but we were sure he was going to be nicer to us than our mother. When Mom was diagnosed with an enlarged heart and told to stop working, she had no choice but to have him take us.

So, we moved in with my father, who was living with a woman in a very tiny four-room house (I was never sure if they were married or co-habitating). They crammed four beds into one room for my sister, two brothers, and me. They had their bedroom from which we could hear their loud lovemaking on a regular basis. His lady, Lucy, was his drinking partner and they often got stupefied. There was a bar down the street where they would regularly hang out. When Lucy got drunk, she would look for ways to set us up to show my father how bad we were. One day, she took her own stockings, cut them up, then claimed we had done it. I can't say that I have ever disliked anyone more in my life–then or since–than Lucy. It was a mutual "hate-hate fest." One day, we got into an argument and I slapped her. My father was off the couch and across the room so fast I never saw him move. I went over his knee, got the spanking of my life, and was thrown out of the house.

My mother came and got me. My brother got thrown out the next week. My sister and other brother ran away two weeks later. We stayed with another of my mother's sisters, Mary, in New York City for a week. She had a very tiny apartment in a brownstone and we were overcrowded. Then the five of us lived in my mother's car for two weeks while my mother tried to figure things out.

Mom bought a mobile home but when she showed up with all her kids, they told her we weren't welcome in the trailer park. So she pulled the trailer out of the park and her boss let her put it in the parking lot of the gas station where she was working. There were no hookups–no electric, no water, no sewer, no heat. We used the dirty, greasy bathroom of the gas station. This didn't go on long before someone in the neighborhood reported our situation to Social Services.

With no choice left to her, my mother went on welfare. It was a shameful thing to accept handouts as she was a strong, independent woman. This was embarrassing for her, but she did it for her children. I was fourteen years old and starting high school. The youngest was just three years old and Mom was finally able to bring him back home from her sister Anne's care.

Those were troubled years for her. By then, we were wild and unruly kids, always getting into trouble. She dealt with drugs, alcohol, theft, arrests, jail, and teenage pregnancy. We borrowed her car and wrecked it. It seemed like she could never get ahead. She'd take one step forward and two steps back. We were, indeed, a handful.

At age sixteen, I got pregnant and went to live in a home for unwed mothers. Our culture severely frowned upon a pregnant woman without a husband back then, calling her all kinds of names and relegating her child to the lowest place in society. Unwed mothers were sent to special homes where they hid until their babies were born, then placed them for adoption and returned home claiming they were away visiting relatives. At least the child would have a chance for a decent life if it got adopted by a loving family.

I wanted to keep that baby so badly. It would love me, and I would love it. It would be my special somebody. My mother told me that if I kept the baby, I could not come back home. I would have to move out on my own.

By that time, we had been on welfare for three years. I was ridiculed at school. No one wanted to be friends with me. The coach refused to let me play on the volleyball team. Because I was poor–from the wrong side of the tracks–people wanted nothing to do with me. I was ashamed. If I kept my baby, I would have to go on welfare. I looked at the baby and thought about his chances in life and how he would be treated. I did not want to be that welfare mother. I wanted better for him and for me. So I put him up for adoption.

Some people take longer to learn life's lessons than others. Two years later, I was pregnant again. It was a little girl this time. Now I was eighteen and of the legal age to keep the baby if I wanted to; I didn't need my mother's permission. But, again, I thought about what we would have together and wanted more for us both. So I placed her for adoption, too.

On my eighteenth birthday, I had gone to the Marine Corps recruiting office and tried to enlist. They took one look at me and told me to go away. I was 4-feet-11 and three-quarter inches and all of ninety-eight pounds. I guess I was just too tiny to be a fierce Marine. I was devastated. I'd wanted to be a Marine ever since I was 8 years old.

Dejected, I took a full-time job as a clerk at the New York State Department of Transportation (DOT) and settled down.

I was dating a boy that I had met when we moved to Islip, New York in 1964. My mother didn't like him and wanted me to break it off. I refused so she threw me out. That was one of my mother's favorite tactics when she got mad at us. She got so good at it that she threw the youngest out when he was just eight years old. She always let us come back though. And she was there whenever you got into trouble. They had to be rough years for her–a single mother with five unruly children bent on self-destruction.

I found a room to rent for a few months, and then found an apartment on the top floor of a two-family house. It was an old building but it suited me just fine. Paul (the boy I refused to break up with) and I got married in 1971 and waited ten years before having our son and another three for our daughter.

We celebrated our fiftieth anniversary in 2021. I smile when I think of that. When we got married, my mother told me we wouldn't last a year. Over the years, I have joked that I stayed married just to spite my mother. By the time she died, I said I had too many years invested to leave. Seriously, I count my lucky stars to have found my soul mate at such a young age (dated at fourteen; married at nineteen). Some people take a lifetime to find the right person; others never do.

During our time together, we got involved with our local church. We taught Sunday school, started a group called ELI (Explore Long Island), and served in various positions on boards and committees. I was certified as a lay speaker and gave many sermons at our local church as well as other churches in the area.

I worked for the DOT for 5 years. As a grade-three clerk, I delivered mail, made copies, filled in on the switchboard, typed, filed, and substituted for the secretary to the department head when she took time off. In high school, I had taken a secretarial track (girls studied to be either secretaries or nurses back then). One day, I went down to the cafeteria and saw a coworker with a recruiting sign for the National Guard on the table in front of him. I stopped to ask some questions on behalf of my husband. The draft was in place then and we were worried he would be called up for Vietnam. My coworker told me that the National Guard had just opened up to women. The conversation at dinner that night went something like, "Guess what I did today?"

I enlisted in the New York Army National Guard (NYARNG) May 1975 and left for three weeks of basic training in November 1975. I had enlisted under a new program called CASP (Civilian Acquired Skills Program). I already had skills I had acquired during my civilian career. The National Guard acknowledged that and required me to take only a very basic course on Army topics. I learned rank, history, military law, how to march and how to salute. When I returned home, I was immediately promoted to E3 private first class.

I served with a helicopter company. It was a weird time. As the only woman in the unit, I was met with both resistance and curiosity. When I walked across the hanger floor, everyone would stop working and just watch me. Conversation stopped when I entered a room. It was like no one had ever seen a woman before. It turned out that aviators are a very superstitious bunch. Women and aircraft are considered to be a bad mix.

I enjoyed my time in the unit and decided I wanted to be a helicopter pilot. The commander would take me flying with him and let me take the stick. He took some time to teach me how to fly a Loach (Hughes OH-6 Cayuse light observation helicopter). It was thrilling and I couldn't wait to fly my own bird. When I asked about putting in an application packet for flight school, I was told I had to have 50 percent of a bachelor's degree completed.

I hated school. The only reason I graduated high school was because my mother had taken me by the ear, marched me to school, and deposited me in the principal's office every day for the last six months of my senior year. Then I had tried community college but dropped out after a month. School. Yuck.

At about the time I enlisted in the National Guard, I accepted a promotion from grade-five stenographer to grade-nine senior stenographer in the New York State Civil Service system. As a result, my name was placed on the promotion list statewide and I was selected to work at the State University of New York/College at Old Westbury (SUNY/COW) in 1975. I worked in the Office of Academic Administration. This is where faculty is hired and where course offerings are decided for the semester.

After several years, I was promoted to grade-twelve administrative assistant, then moved from the Civil Service Employees Association (CSEA) to the United University Professions (UUP) where I became part of the professional university ranks during my time at Old Westbury. It was very enjoyable and challenging work and I stayed at Old Westbury for eleven years, until I had my daughter in 1984 (my son was born in 1981 and I had taken a leave of absence for one year before returning to work). When I left to care for my children, I began teaching college classes at night as a way to stay home with them during the day.

So I went to school at night to get a bachelor's degree. I was lucky enough to qualify for life experience credits, so I wound up getting a four-year degree in four years going to school part-time at night. Once I'd finished 50 percent of a bachelor's degree, I raised the issue of applying for flight school again. Now I was told I had to be a commissioned officer to qualify for entrance to flight school. So I signed up for Officer Candidate School at the New York State Empire Military Academy (ESMA). I went to drill in Upstate New York (a two-and-a-half-hour drive one way) for a year. The training kicked off with two weeks and ended with two weeks at the academy, with classes every third weekend in-between. That was a challenging time. I was working full-time, going to school at night, and taking officer training. On top of that we bought a new house. I remember moving everything in and then kissing my husband good-bye and going off for weekend training, leaving him to find places for all our stuff.

It was a proud day in 1979 when I graduated OCS and was pinned as a second lieutenant. I was finally able to file an application for flight school.

It was rejected because I was too short. I felt like I had been gut punched.

Apparently, there was a minimum-height requirement that no one had bothered to tell me about. I had worked so hard to meet all the requirements and still, I got turned away.

I transferred from the National Guard to the Army Reserve and wound up serving a total of thirty-one years in the military (five in the National Guard and twenty-six in the Army Reserve). I was mobilized four times: in 1979 for a strike by New York State prison guards; in 1992 for Operation Desert Storm; in 2001 for the attack on the World Trade Center; and in 2005, when I was sent overseas for a year in support of Operation Iraqi Freedom. I retired at the rank of O5 lieutenant colonel with more than forty ribbons and medals awarded over the life of my career to include the Bronze Star, three Meritorious Service Medals and five Army Commendation Medals.

From 1992 to 1996, I worked as an office manager at the State University of New York at Stony Brook in the Department of Parking & Transportation Services. I had the best time, working with a great staff. I loved my boss.

At that time, there was a great deal of pressure to get cars off the road. We established a ride share program, offering reserved parking spaces for those who carpooled to work. It seems like every college builds its campus and then says, "Parking? What parking?" There is never enough parking on a college campus and reserved sites are highly desirable. I also helped to manage four parking garages and sixty-two parking lots. During my time in this position, I enrolled in a professional certification program as a parking professional and earned certification just as the university disbanded the department. I was let go.

In 1996, I accepted a position as the manager of an off-airport parking lot in Orlando, Florida. It was an interesting assignment. It was a brand-new facility that was being built from the ground up. The owners of the facility were three gentlemen from Georgia–a lawyer, an accountant, and an entrepreneur. They had pooled their money together as an investment.

I arrived in May, got the place staffed and opened for the July Fourth weekend, and worked until October. I hired all the employees and trained and supervised them.

The parking facility was not making the money the partners expected, so they decided to bring in a management company after five months. I refused to work with them, stating that I had a contract to work directly with the owners. They decided to terminate my assignment. My husband had arrived a week earlier with all our household goods and a sales contract in hand to sell our house (he and our children had remained in New York to get the house ready for sale). Thankfully, we had not signed the contract and were able to return to our house in New York. Our joke is that the furniture took a vacation to Florida.

As you might imagine, I was sorely depressed for a while after we were back home. No matter the reason you are fired from a job, it is still humiliating. I was let go not because I did anything wrong but because I would not accept the new working arrangement.

Back home, I hunted for a full-time job back in the civil service sector. I had a great résumé. About 95 percent of the time, I got an interview when I applied for a job but just wasn't getting hired. I went back to work as an adjunct professor teaching college courses part-time. At first, I taught statistics but over the years I was able to expand my offerings to include other business courses like organizational behavior, management theory, business communication, management behavior, and freshman orientation. I had contracts with both a community college and a four-year college. By the time I retired I had taught for more than 28 years.

In 2002, I decided to go back to school to get a doctoral degree. (I should note that after completing my bachelor's degree, I went on to earn an MBA. I discovered that I actually liked going to school.) So, I enrolled at Dowling College in Oakdale, New York. It was an accelerated program whereby students earned their degrees in just three years instead of the usual seven. At the beginning of my third year in 2005, the Army sent me to the Middle East for a year in support of Operation Iraqi Freedom. After I returned home, it took me a year to get back on track. Then I couldn't find a suitable topic to research. I wound up taking seven years to earn my EdD in higher education administration. Ironic, huh?

After I returned from my tour in Iraq/Kuwait/Afghanistan, my husband, Paul, told me I was eligible to join the American Legion. I had no idea what that was. I went to a meeting at the local post and was promptly elected to the position of chaplain (they wanted to make me the commander but I refused because I knew nothing about them). After a year and a half, I did become commander and served for six years. I was both the first woman commander and the longest-serving commander at Rusy-Bohm Post 411.

In 2009, I was hired as the office manager in the Teaching, Learning & Technology Department at Stony Brook University. It was a turbulent time fraught with political nonsense and petty rivalries. My boss wound up leaving and I was moved to another department. After three years, I decided to put in my retirement papers. In 2012, I walked away from the working world and have never looked back.

In 2013, my husband and I turned the keys to the house over to our daughter and her husband. We climbed into our fifth-wheel RV and took off to explore America. We have been living on the road ever since. We've been fortunate to have seen every state from Alaska to Florida. We have made many friends around the country and enjoy visiting as we arrive in an area where they live.

In 2017, I was diagnosed with small lymphocytic lymphoma (SLL). The doctor told me that it was a very slow growing cancer and often takes years before any action is needed. So we adopted a wait-and-see approach. I went to the doctor regularly for bloodwork and scans between trips around the country. Finally, in 2019, the doctor told me one node had grown large enough to impinge on my bladder. It was time to start treatment. We returned to New York where I have been working with a doctor at Memorial Sloan Kettering Cancer Center. I have been on chemotherapy since September of 2019. It's one pill a day and appears to be working beautifully. I return every three months for follow up and thus far–knock on wood–the nodes have been shrinking and things seem to be under control.

In 2020, I was contacted by the principal's office at the high school where I graduated fifty-one years earlier. They wanted to include me in the Islip High School Hall of Fame Induction Class for 2020-21 as a distinguished graduate for academic and career accomplishments. Unfortunately, the COVID-19 pandemic caused the homecoming parade and induction ceremony to be postponed. In July 2021, they again contacted me to resume the induction process. What an honor to be recognized with a lifetime award! Especially since I was such an unremarkable student when I walked out those doors so many years ago.

So here we are, as I write this, in 2022. We just came through the worst viral contagion in our lifetime. Yet Paul and I still managed to travel around the country. Continuing with my desire to be in leadership positions (remember my life-changing event?), we have stepped up to serve as wagon masters in our travel club. We joined Special Military Active Recreational Travelers (SMART) in 2014 and since then have gone on four caravans and led two others (one around Utah and the other around Upstate New York). We look forward to many more years of RVing around the United States. We are now in the "zone" (as I call it) and we don't know how much longer we will enjoy this mortal life. Until it's time to go, we intend to make the most of it. As I like to say, I'm going to live forever or die trying.

GOLDEN NUGGETS

Never ignore a barking dog. This has become something of a mantra in our house but actually started with a camping trip. We were camped in our pop-up trailer. It was small and couldn't fit all our food as well as the four of us with the dog. So we put our coolers with two weeks' worth of groceries and baby formula outside beside the camper, just as we had done on dozens of previous campouts. Later that night, our dog was barking furiously. We figured she was barking at a raccoon or deer in the area and shushed her. The next morning, we went out to get food from the cooler only to find it gone. When we reported it to the rangers, they said they had been having trouble with gypsies in the area. We were stunned! If they had told us about this issue, we would have been more vigilant. As it is, when a dog barks (i.e., when a problem is obvious), go see what's happening.

You always have a choice. You may not like the choices you have, but you always have a choice. Even deciding to do nothing is a choice.

You are never alone. There are always agencies and people around who want to help. Sometimes you have to hunt for them but they are there. Don't lose hope. Don't give up. They're out there and they want to help.

Adversity builds character. Don't be in such a hurry to "save" someone from difficulty. Some of the greatest people I know tell stories of being horrific teenagers. They did things that I would find appalling if my children had done them. My son's godfather was a wonderful person. But he used to tell stories of how he stole his father's car and went speeding around the neighborhood, got into fights, did a lot of drinking, and was arrested twice. He was probably what I would call a "bad teen." Yet he was able to get past all that and by the time we met him, he had gone on to become a great man. If your teen gets arrested, let them spend the night in jail. When they are assigned a project, make sure they do it all in good fashion and on time. Hold their feet to the fire.

How good something tastes is directly proportional to how hungry you are. When I was in the National Guard, we were flying a mission to Upstate New York in January. We picked up ice on the rotor blades and were forced to make an emergency landing at a small airport. The pilot was directed to a large empty hangar where we had to wait it out. It was late (after midnight), we were starving, and cold. Someone came by and stated that there was some take-out left over in the office. They were cold hamburgers with mustard on them. We gobbled them up. At any other time, I would have pushed it away with an "ugh," but right then, it was the best thing I had ever tasted in my life. I have tried several times since then to recreate the taste sensation of those burgers but could never tolerate it enough to take more than one bite.

You are always more popular when you are in a place of power–either through money or by position. When I was in Officer Candidate School, we rotated serving in key positions. I was assigned to serve as the first sergeant. During my "day on the hot seat," I found that I was a very popular person. Everyone seemed to want to be near me, to talk to me about the plans for the day, to be part of the leadership group.

Later on, I became the commandant of a headquarters company (HHC) in a support group. Again, I was suddenly a very popular person. People sought me out for advice, to share information, to include me in planning functions and important meetings. I left the HHC and went on to become a member of the Inspector General (IG) Office in an Army Reserve HQ. This was an even more important position, and one of considerable power. The office is treated with a great deal of respect and deference. The IG is authorized to go over the commanding general's head direct to Washington, DC, if necessary. Everything handled in the office is sensitive and confidential and treated on a need-to-know basis. The staff can go into any unit, any office, any place in the command and look at anything and speak to anyone.

These were incredibly heady experiences. I can see how a position of power can go to someone's head–why presidents and kings feel invincible. If in a position like this, it takes a great deal of self-discipline and awareness to control innate tendencies to abuse the office and look for special treatment; to be held above the law. For example, George Washington was an incredible individual because he did not take advantage of his standing in a newly formed nation.

A weak person is a helpless person. I read a report that said 50 percent of the people in nursing homes are there simply because they are too weak to care for themselves. Keep yourself physically fit enough to take care of your personal needs. Do some exercise every day. There is no more wonderful feeling than one of physical fitness.

Treat your children with dignity and respect. They are the future. I once read a sign outside a local church that said, "If you plant weeds, don't expect flowers to grow." It is your job as a parent to prepare your child for adulthood. That requires that you teach them how to live and work in a civilized society. Treat every interaction as an opportunity to teach.

Treat the elderly with dignity and respect. They carry the memories of our history; they are the link to the past. I just love talking with old people (these days, they are peers). They recount amazing stories of their childhoods at a time when life was less complicated. I have also learned a lot about our history and culture as a nation. For example, my uncle used to complain about leaded gas. When he was young, they charged extra at the gas pump because (they claimed) they added lead to the fuel. Years later, they charged more because they were taking the lead out (this was when unleaded gas was becoming popular). He swore it was all a scam. Today, all gas is unleaded (or so they tell us).

Look for the humor in every situation. It seems to me that learning to laugh at situations actually extends your life. Anecdotally, I believe people with a good sense of humor live longer. Look at George Burns, Jerry Lewis, Carol Burnett, Dick Van Dyke, Betty White, etc. Comedians certainly seem to live longer. Is it because they find humor in life?

Self-talk is an important tool for self-discovery, self-soothing, and self-education.

Continuously seek to learn something new. There is so much to learn about the world around us. Today's children will know more than we ever did. There is so much data available in easily accessible forms. Curiosity keeps you interested in life. People with a broad knowledge base are very interesting to talk to.

Love the world around you. Respect nature. Be mindful of the fragility of the earth. Work to do everything you can to minimize your impact on it. Recycle. Use resources frugally. Everyone should know how to take a Navy shower.

Always have an animal in your house. This is another anecdotal observation on my part. It seems that people who have grown up with an animal in the house are more tolerant and accepting of others who are different. This is not to say that anyone who didn't have an animal is less tolerant or that everyone who had an animal in their house is more tolerant, but *in general*, people who had, and still have, pets seem to be more accepting of the differences between people.

Travel. The best way to end bigotry is to travel around and meet people from other areas. You very quickly learn that people are more similar than dissimilar. We may have different cultural beliefs and ceremonies, but everyone wants to live in peace and be able to raise their family in safety with enough food and shelter to be healthy and secure.

Chicken soup really does make you feel better when you're sick.

No plan survives first contact. There's a saying: "Life is what happens to you while you are making other plans." While you are making your plans, people on the other side are also making their plans. When these plans clash, things can become chaotic. Be flexible and expect things to go wrong.

People thought Napoleon Bonaparte was psychic because he always seemed to know what the enemy was going to do and knew how to react to it. When interviewed, Bonaparte said that he simply tried to anticipate every scenario that could happen and developed a plan to react to it before going into battle.

The world is no longer a singular experience. It is global. No longer are people born, grow up, and die in the same little town. They say that a person will have an average of twelve jobs in their lifetime. With the click of a button, you can virtually travel to just about anywhere in the world.

Take your children on business trips with you. Teach them how to travel. When I went on a business trip, I would leave my child in the hotel room and give him or her assignments to do. I'd have them find a rental car, check out the bus schedules, find out the movie times, etc. Help them learn to navigate the world.

Don't let the little things prevent you from enjoying the big things in life. I went to a dinner on the Intrepid in New York City. It was a dress uniform event and guests included Mr. and Mrs. Avery Fisher as well as General and Mrs. Colin Powell. As we came into the dining area, there was a receiving line. The first person I met was General Barker. Now, you have to understand my relationship with this general. For some reason, every time I got around this man, I behaved like an idiot. I don't know why, but he just had that kind of effect on me.

The first time I met him was at a party my boss, Colonel Edmundson, was having at Fort Totten. I had just taken a handful of peanuts from a dish when the colonel brought the general over and introduced me to him. I was so taken with meeting a general that I immediately offered my hand without taking the nuts out of it. The general very graciously gave a perfunctory shake of my monkey paw. After that, every time I saw the guy, I would say something stupid, fall over something, or just come off as the most disheveled or uncoordinated person in the world. I'm sure he wondered how I ever got on his staff.

Anyway, I came through the door, and the first person on the receiving line was General Barker. He shook my hand and asked me if I was an MP or an IG. I mumbled my answer, thinking that I had somehow put my collar brass on wrong. Now, I'm in this long line and people are pushing behind me to keep going. I would have loved to step out of the line to check my brass but there was no way to do that. So I kept trying to surreptitiously get a look at the brass on my collar as we shuffled through the line. I tried to be nonchalant about it– I didn't want anyone to think that I didn't know how to put the brass on my uniform. It didn't matter anyway, because I wouldn't have been able fix it then and there, but I was obsessed with knowing if my insignia was on correctly. Why had General Barker said that?

I came to the next couple, an elderly gentleman and woman. They happened to be Avery Fisher and his wife. But

I was so busy trying to figure out if my brass was on right that I didn't really focus on them. I gave a superficial hello and pushed along. Then there was the next couple, a pleasant looking Black man and woman. Again, I gave a brief nod and handshake but didn't really take notice of them. Suddenly, I was through the receiving line, and I never really made meaningful contact with anyone. And there was nothing wrong with my brass after all.

I could imagine General Powell and General Barker talking after the party and Powell saying, "There was this strange, young officer on the line who was busy looking at her collar instead of me." And General Barker replying, "That would have to be Thomas. That woman is strange!"

The point is that I spent precious time focusing on something I could not change. At that point, my brass was on my uniform the way it was. There was no doing anything about it. I should have just left it and concentrated on greeting the very special people I had come to meet.

(Just a note about my uniform. The dress blue uniform in the US Army has a color stripe on the arm that matches the branch of service that officer is assigned to. The brass on your collar should correspond to the color of the stripe. I was an MP on temporary assignment to the IG office. Normally, I wore MP brass that matched the color stripe on my sleeve. I didn't know the IG was a branch or that it had a color, too, so I never changed the stripe on my dress blues. I had gone to the event with IG brass on my collar and MP stripe on my sleeve. Just another goof for General Barker to shake his head over.)

It's just another eagle. Something you see all the time can stop seeming special. We took a cruise to Alaska. During that cruise, we were on the lookout for all kinds of wildlife, especially the kind you don't normally see around your home. We saw lots of eagles, something we had never seen except in zoos. We saw so many eagles, in fact, that by the end of the trip when someone would point out an eagle, we would say, "Oh, it's just another eagle." Today, we say "It's just another eagle" to indicate that something seems ordinary and plentiful.

The United States of America is the greatest country in the world. Is it perfect? No. There are things that could be improved but it is still better than anywhere else. Did you know that over 1 million people take the oath of citizenship every year? Some of these people were asked why they wanted to be American citizens. What was it about America that made them want to leave their own country and adopt this one? The answers were astounding and eye-opening.

One man said they have running water in America. The interviewer asked, "Didn't you have water in your country?" The man answered, "Yes, we had water, but I had to get it four or five times a day at the local well." Another person said he liked 9-1-1. "You just call 9-1-1 and someone comes and saves you." For him, that was a marvelous thing being able to call someone you didn't know and they would rush to your aid, even risking their own life to save yours. Another man said that when he came to America, he saw a man walking his dog with socks on its feet. He asked why the dog was wearing socks. The owner told him the pavement was hot and he didn't want his dog to hurt its feet. The immigrant, who was from Iraq, marveled at the fact that we would be so considerate of an animal. He said, "I would come to this country as an animal because they are treated better here than people in my country are treated." A woman from Slovakia observed that Americans are always complaining about everything. They complain about their government. They complain about their jobs. They complain about their children. They complain about their parents. They complain about their clothes, their houses, their pets, their neighbors, the cops. They just don't appreciate what they have. She said that if you complained in her country, they would kill you.

Hope is not a plan.

People are more likely to believe something if it appears in writing. When I counseled employees about issues at work, I would tell them that the first time would be verbal, kind of like a Dutch Uncle talk. If things didn't get better, the second counseling would be in writing. I can't tell you how many times that first talk was ignored but the session recorded in writing had a profound effect. There's something permanent about putting things in writing. People will believe it if it's in writing, more so than if they just hear it.

It doesn't hurt to ask. If the answer is no, you're no worse off than you were because you didn't have it to start with. But if the answer is yes, then you have gained something you did not have before. All just by asking for it. You lose nothing by asking for the things you want.

The most ordinary thing becomes precious once it's taken away. Joni Mitchell sang a song that brings this home. "They took all the trees and put them in a tree museum. Then they charged the people a dollar and a half to see 'em . . .. Don't it always seem to go that you don't know what you've got 'til it's gone. They paved paradise and put up a parking lot."

Guilt, remorse and regret are generally useless emotions. Well, let me rephrase that. _Long-term_ guilt, remorse, and regret should not be allowed under normal circumstances. Short-term, immediate feelings are important to alerting you to the fact that you did something wrong–broke a rule, hurt someone's feelings, did something wrong. You should then fix it, make it right, atone for it, then get on with life. Carrying those feelings around for years just drags you down and wastes precious energy, like a weight around your heart. It is useless to feel sorry about something you did in the past because you cannot change it. All the worry and regret you can bring to bear still will not undo what you did. Make it right and get on with your life.

All that's required for bad things to happen is for good people to do nothing. A young woman was being attacked in New York City. She screamed for help. Over a hundred people witnessed the incident. If someone had yelled at the guy, either telling him to stop or that they were going to call the police, it might have stopped the attack. A witness didn't even have to say anything. Just call the police. Not one person in the group, neighbor or passerby, bothered to do anything. They did not yell at the guy. They didn't try to intervene. They didn't call the police. As a result, the young woman was raped and killed.

When you stand around with your hands in your pockets or turn your back, you let bad things happen. If you see something wrong, step forward and say something. Stand up for your principles and the safety of others around you. Do not allow people to abuse animals, children, or other people. Stop it if you can. If not, report it to the proper agency.

Communication is power. The most important skills in life are reading, writing, and speaking. If you can communicate with everyone in a way that is easily understandable, you have a very powerful skill. You need these skills in so many situations in life: at work, in college, during marriage, with children, etc.

Volunteerism is essential to society's success. We can't depend on the government to take care of everything we need as a society. A civilized society depends on its members to take care of one another. Government regulations are established to manage a general populace. There are many people who fall into the cracks and can't be helped because of regulations. Thank goodness for churches that provide food banks for those who don't qualify for welfare or clinics that provide free care to those who have no health insurance or after-school programs that provide caretakers for children who have working parents. Volunteer to do something in your town. Work at the local hospital or animal shelter, serve with a fraternal association like the boy or girl scouts, help out at a homeless shelter, etc. You get the picture. Give a couple of hours a week to make your community a better place.

Read every day. Reading expands horizons and increases communication skills. When I first started dating, a boy told me I was pretty to look at but the minute I opened my mouth, I ruined the effect. He was talking about my poor grammar. Luckily, I am an avid reader. As time went by, my vocabulary expanded and improved, and I was better able to hold a discussion in a "civilized manner." When I first started college, I was told I needed a remedial writing course. By the end of the four years, I passed the test without ever taking such a class. Just by reading and paying attention to the people around me.

Accept everyone as they are, not as you want them to be. The world would be such a boring place if everyone was the same. Different styles, different beliefs, different behaviors are the things that make life so interesting. Embrace the differences and learn to appreciate them.

No one is useless or unnecessary. Everyone has a place on this earth and an importance in the greater scheme of things. Never label yourself as "just a . . . *something*." Even the janitors at NASA, when asked what they do, reply that they help put a rocket on the moon. Their role is just as important in the overall scheme of things as the engineer's role. Don't ever underestimate your role in life. The job wouldn't be there if it wasn't needed. You are needed.

All dogs bite. This has also become a mantra in our house; again, inspired by our dog (our animals provide great inspiration to us). It is in a dog's nature to bite. It explores the world with its mouth–watch a puppy learn about a new thing. It licks you when it's happy and bites when it feels threatened. Any dog will bite if pushed to its limits. This has come to mean that if you know a person's disposition to be disagreeable, don't be surprised when they do something you don't like. It's in their nature.

Look for the good things in every situation. As we go through life, we experience many ups and downs–what I like to refer to as the troughs and waves of life. Focusing on the bad things only drags you down and makes you miss the good things in life. Every situation, no matter how bad, is better than it could be. Look for the good in the situation and focus on it. Let it sustain and carry you through the trough until you can get back on top of the wave again. It will make the situation seem less dire, and the time will go much quicker.

If you don't like who you are, change it. We all spend a certain amount of time blaming our parents for who we are. But at some point–usually at eighteen years of age–you become responsible for yourself. There is no one else to blame for who or what you are at that point. If you do not like the way you turned out, then do something about it. It won't happen overnight. It may take years of therapy. The sooner you get started and keep at it, the sooner the change will take place.

I was filled with self-loathing by the time I reached adulthood. I hated everyone, but most of all myself. That made me very unhappy, so I started to see a psychologist. I was in therapy for ten years. During that time, I learned to understand myself and my motivations. I credit that therapist with saving me and helping me to build an incredible life which had been unimaginable in my childhood.

Give 100 percent to your job. Sometimes we are forced to take a job we don't really want or like because it's all we can find at the time. Regardless, if you agree to take a job then the employer has the right to expect you to do the best you can. Whether you work as a ditch digger or a teacher or a house cleaner, give your whole effort to being the best you can be at that job. You may eventually move on to another, more desirable job. Let your previous boss sing your praises.

If you want to believe in something but can't make yourself do it, live as if you do, and the belief will come. My husband and I began to attend church when we got married. I would look at some of the other parishioners praying and wish fervently that I could believe as firmly as they did. They would sit with their eyes closed and faces upturned with a look of peace on their faces. They looked connected somehow. Oh, how I wanted that, too. But try as I might, I could not make myself believe that there really is a God who sits in heaven listening to my prayers. This ate me up inside and made me think I was unsaveable. Then one day it dawned on me. *Okay, so you can't believe in God. But you CAN believe in the teachings of a Christian life. Live by the Ten Commandments–don't steal, don't lie, don't kill, respect one another, follow the golden rule, etc.–and you will be doing God's bidding.* I began to do that and somehow, over the years, I came to believe in a higher being. I don't know when it happened; it just did.

41

The only one who can change a person is that person. I've heard it said that a man marries a woman hoping she will never change and a woman marries a man thinking he will change. People act certain ways because of their beliefs in the world around them. You might not like someone's behavior but you will not convince them to change unless they want to change.

New York City provides a great example of this. We live on Long Island, about fifty miles east of the city. Driving into the city is a big hassle–traffic, congestion, narrow streets, lack of parking, fear of damage to your car, etc. If I go into New York City, I will take the train because I do not want to deal with all the issues that cause stress and possible damage to my car. My husband, on the other hand, always wants to have his car at hand so he will drive into the city and deal with all the problems of big city driving. I changed my driving behavior because I did not want to deal with all the negative issues of driving in a big city. My husband did not change because he likes to have his vehicle available to him, despite all the issues of big-city driving. Deaf to my urgings, he has not changed his driving habits.

Place relationships above money. Money is only a tool to be used to give you life, not the life itself. When faced with a choice between money and relationships, choose your family and friends, unless it would cost you your job or cause an important loss in your workplace. The job is important, yes.

There is no denying it. We all need the income, and sometimes we have to work when we'd rather not. But when you have a choice, always go for the relationship.

Money is made to be spent.

Don't assume how people are going to react to you. When I decided to retire from my job, I was afraid to tell my boss. I dreaded all the yelling and screaming that was sure to follow my announcement. We had been going through a number of big changes in the office. First, a new president took over at the university. He hired a consultant firm to evaluate operations to find more efficient and cheaper ways to do business. Soon after the first recommendation came out, the head of my division retired. Then my boss resigned. One of the consultant's recommendations was that they take all the people with like duties and pool them in one group rather than working in individual departments. I was the budget and personnel manager in my department. As a result of this review, I was moved to a pool of budget people in the business office. Now, I not only supported my department, but also shared my talents with other departments throughout the division. If that wasn't enough, both the university and New York State decided to move to new financial systems. This meant implementing new programs and procedures for processing purchase orders. On top of that, the consultants also recommended a move to a new email service. My department had changed email programs less than two years before. We hadn't fully recovered from the last change and were now struggling to master this new one. There had been lots of changes and moves in the previous year. My new boss went from operating with a staff of three to an office of twelve people. We were having planning meetings daily on how responsibilities and duties were going to be split up and many brainstorming sessions on how to set up operations, what forms to use, and so on.

So it was with great trepidation that I finally decided to announce my retirement. I was sure my boss would be angry with me. After *all* the planning, *all* the meetings, *all* the procedures we put into place, *now* I was going to walk out as we started the new fiscal year. Boy, she was going to be mad at me! I imagined the most awful teeth-gnashing, chest-beating, hair-pulling reaction that has ever taken place in the business world.

The union required thirty to ninety days' notice of retirement. I figured forty-five days was good. The closer it got to the day I'd planned my announcement, the more anxious I got. This was going to be so hard. I couldn't sleep and suffered terrible stomach aches.

I had to be strong. I walked into the office on Monday morning and blurted out, "I'm retiring next month." My boss was walking by and replied, "Yeah, we'd all like to retire from this place." She thought I was making a joke. When I didn't come back at her, she stopped, looked at me, and said, "Wait, are you joking or serious?" I told her when my last day of work would be. She got quiet and walked away. No name calling, no yelling, no scene. The rest of the office erupted in a frenzy! Everyone within hearing distance came running over to congratulate me. As the word spread around the building, then the department, the division, and finally the university, I got calls, visits, and emails from loads of people congratulating me and wishing me well. People I didn't know were coming up to me and shaking my hand. It was as if I'd won the lottery and everyone wanted a part of it.

I thought my coworkers were going to be angry with me because I was leaving in the middle of reorganization and new processes. I couldn't believe the difference in reactions from what I expected to what actually happened. As for my boss, she later asked me, "Is it something I said?" When I told her it was just the right time to go, she confessed that she had to keep working two and a half more years before she could retire. She was also counting down the time. I don't think she was happy about my leaving–my position would probably be empty for about a year before a replacement was hired–but she was not angry with me. She seemed resigned to the fact that I had the right to go and she would just have to accept it.

I was amazed at how this all played out. I was worried sick about it being such a negative thing and it turned out to be an extremely positive experience. Somehow, in my mind, I had played it up to be terrible. All because I assumed my boss and coworkers would be angry.

How many times have we worried about giving someone bad news because we were afraid of their reaction? Can't tell Mom about the bad grade in school because she's going to ground me for life. Can't tell Dad about crashing the car because he's going to kill me. Can't tell my wife about losing my job because she's going to leave me. Can't tell my boss about the missed deadline because she's going to fire me. We fill ourselves with anxiety and imagine the worst possible scenarios. And while we do sometimes get yelled at, and maybe somebody stops talking to somebody for a few days, or some privileges get taken away, it's usually never as bad as we think it's going to be. Imagination is a wonderful thing to have–but it's a two-edged sword. We need it to be creative and invent new things, but it can cause us to create monsters in our minds, to imagine things as much worse than they really are.

Don't judge a book by its cover. This was brought home when a new lieutenant colonel (LTC) was assigned to the IG office. He had been forced upon the office by the commanding general. None of us liked the new guy and were very suspicious of his motives. At first, the LTC looked slick and evil. After getting to know him and finding he was a warm, empathetic, loving human being, he actually became attractive. The transformation was amazing! The staff came to respect and like him very much. Give people a chance to prove they are decent folks.

Take the time to form your own impressions of people. I reported to the colonel for my new assignment as the operations officer for a training battalion. We talked about my section, its purview, and my responsibilities. Near the end of our conversation, he stated that one of the officers in my section had been irresponsible and he wanted me to fire him. I promised that I would evaluate the individual and his contributions to the section.

As it turned out, the former chief of the section (my predecessor) had favored his assistant to the detriment of other officers in the section. The individual I was told to fire turned out to be disenchanted with the section. He had not been given substantial responsibility. He was excluded from important meetings and treated somewhat disrespectfully. I began to give him important assignments and to include him in all staff meetings as one of the officers in my section. He quickly displayed remarkable skills and great analytical insight. Within the year, I appointed him as my assistant. He worked for me for years, not only in the training battalion but also when I invited him to join me when I transferred to another unit. If I had listened to the people who advised me about him when I first arrived, I would have lost a valuable asset. Make up your own mind about people.

Teach your children to delay gratification. Expecting instant rewards creates frustration. Learning to wait for a reward teaches children patience and perseverance, and helps them to grow up happier and more successful in life. It gives them skills for working diligently toward goals. This is an essential trait to have in the business world where you have to work your way up the ladder.

Have a mantra that motivates and compliments you. When my husband and I have a glass of wine, we clink glasses and one of us says, "Here's to another day in paradise." To which the other one replies, "With you." It's not because we live on some exotic island in the Bahamas. We don't have a secret hideaway in the mountains. Even though we are living our dream of traveling around the United States, it's not perfect. We still have to clean house, do laundry, go food shopping, and empty the cat box. Yet we know that we are responsible for our own happiness. That happiness comes from your attitude about your situation. I've seen people with beautiful homes who were unhappy and people with very little who were happy.

My sister has a saying inked on her mirror that says, "You are beautiful." It's not to remind her about physical beauty but of her inner beauty. The mantra reminds her of her devotion to bring peace and love to the people around her. Your outlook on life determines your level of happiness.

There is no perfect relationship, nor is there a perfect person. In our fantasy relationships, no one is angry; there is no poverty, illness, depression, or death. These things do happen in real life, however, and their presence causes us to change the way we interact with others. In addition, the first blush of a new relationship often blots out the less desirable side of a person. It is not until we have spent a considerable amount of time with someone that we discover that he scratches his private parts in public, or that she never picks up after herself, or that he belches during meals, or that she has a petty, spiteful side. Whatever the shortcoming, we all have them. Accept each other's humanness and focus instead on what you like about that person.

"Why" is the most powerful word in the English language. It challenges. It educates. It explores. It explains. When I was eight years old, I asked my mother "Why?" in response to something she told me to do. She responded with an explanation to which I again asked "Why?" It continued that way until she finally ended with an exasperated "Because God made it that way!" That was fascinating to me! After that, I asked "Why?" for everything and the answer always eventually came back to "That's the way it is!" As an adult, I often ask why something is the way it is because I want to fully understand the situation. Never be afraid to question something so you can fully comprehend what's happening.

Things could always be worse. I read a poem about a man who was complaining about having no shoes. Then he met a man with no feet. That has been a kind of driving force for me. No matter how bad you think your situation is, it could *always* be worse.

A trust betrayed can never be recaptured. Trust is such a fragile thing. Once it has been earned, it is a treasure to have knowing that someone trusts you to be who you are. All it takes is one small indiscretion to lose that trust. And once gone, the mistrust is always there. A doubt will linger forever.

Cultivate a cheerful and optimistic outlook on life.

Dress for the job you want, not the one you have. When I first started working at the New York State Department of Transportation as a grade-three clerk, I didn't think I had to dress up for work. After all, I just delivered the mail, sat at the switchboard, did filing, made copies and didn't really interact with anyone in any important way (or so I thought) I was the lowest of the low in the department. A kind and wise coworker took me aside and asked if I wanted to get promoted to a higher grade. He asked how high a grade I wanted to go. When I confessed that I wanted to make a very high grade, he advised me to dress for that job. He said that even though I didn't work directly for the people I supported, they still saw me performing my job and made judgements based on my appearance. He told me to give them the impression I was an up and coming professional. From that point on, I dressed professionally and was often mistaken for someone of a higher rank simply because of my attire.

Don't make a major decision when extreme emotions are at play. We were looking for a new RV. I had been scouring the internet searching for the exact fifth-wheel RV that we wanted. Finally, the model we were looking for popped up for sale and we quickly made an offer to buy it. I called the salesman in Arizona and told him we wanted the RV. We were in Florida and drove to Arizona to get it. When we arrived, we found the RV was the model we wanted but they had taken it to RV shows where it had been treated badly and damaged. We got into a disagreement with the salesman and things got pretty heated. The manager didn't want to give us back our deposit. As a result, we did not take the RV. But we had just rushed over a thousand miles to get what we thought was the perfect camper.

Feeling flushed from our argument and high on the desire to buy a new RV, we drove down the road, pulled into another dealership, and bought a different model fifth-wheel RV (not the one we wanted). It turned out to be a terrible purchase. On our drive back to Florida, we made a list of all the things that were wrong with the RV. By the time we arrived in Florida, we had two pages of deficiencies on it. We wound up trading that RV for a different fifth-wheel RV. It cost us financially but we were not willing to keep the bad RV with all its deficiencies. It was an expensive lesson.

Stop and take a breath before plunging into a situation, especially where large amounts of money are involved.

Everyone should do something for their country. We are the people. We make our country what we want it to be. Join the military, serve in the Peace Corps or Americorps, be a missionary on a reservation, etc. Be a servant to your country and it will be great. Everyone, regardless of their abilities, can and should give at least two years to a cause that helps others.

If you are feeling lost and unsure of what to do with your life, think about joining the military. During the three and a half years I served in the IG Office, I interviewed hundreds of people. I can't tell you how many times I spoke with a senior NCO or officer and heard the same story: "There I was, 17/18 years old, standing in front of the judge. He told me it's the Army or jail. I enlisted and it made all the difference in the world."

Those men found routine, discipline, and a career when they were lost and foundering teenagers. Even if you don't go on to serve your entire career in the armed forces, you will gain skills in both job performance and personal interaction during your service. You will also have the opportunity to earn a college education for free.

Spend at least one day a week alone with your spouse, without the kids or parents or friends–just the two of you. Your children will grow up and leave the house one day. That will leave the two of you alone to continue your life together. Make sure that you don't grow apart over the years while tending to the children and your jobs. Have a date night. Stay connected.

Be constructive in conflict. Address the issue or the behavior; don't attack the person. When arguing with someone, it would be so easy to just call them names or tell them they're stupid and just don't understand. That would not be very productive in resolving the argument. Use "I" words rather than "you" words like "*I feel uncomfortable with ...*" rather than "*You make me feel uncomfortable with ...*" The "you" word is like wagging a finger in someone's face. It is accusatory.

Everyone makes mistakes. Don't beat yourself up. Fix them and move on. Forgive others their mistakes.

***Kiss, hug, and confirm your love for your spouse, children, and loved ones every* day**. Everything can change in the blink of an eye–disease, accident, disability, death. Every year, more than 38,000 people across the USA leave their homes and never return. They get into their cars to drive somewhere and die in an accident. How many times have you glibly told someone good-bye, fully expecting to see them later? Or worse, didn't even acknowledge their goodbye because you were watching TV or reading something? Be sure that the last thing they hear from you is kind and loving.

Every generation makes its own mistakes. You don't repeat your parents' mistakes; you make new ones. No one is perfect. Kids refuse to come with instruction manuals. Adults are left to fumble their way through parenthood, trying to do their best to raise their children to be responsible, productive members of society. Forgive your parents their shortcomings. Don't be too hard on yourself.

Don't hold grudges. Let go of negative feelings that would pull you down. Carrying a grudge is like wearing a stone around your neck. Every time you think about that person, you stop and swear about them. "Oh, that guy (or gal) really makes me so mad!" Now you are filled with negative feelings and that person doesn't even know it. They are not affected at all but that moment has been ruined for you. Forgive that person for whatever wrong they did to you and move on. Life is too short to let someone short circuit your enjoyment for years.

Walk away from a heated situation until you cool down. When I was growing up and my mother got angry, she would say "I can't wait until you kids grow up and get out!" As an adult, I can understand her frustration. She was a single parent with five unruly children who taxed her patience frequently. Unfortunately, as a child, I interpreted her outburst to mean she didn't love me. That she was keeping me there only because the law said she had to, not because she wanted me.

You don't want to do or say something you will regret later. Some people think they can just let loose with their anger then apologize later as though that would erase everything. Each time you say something mean to someone, it's like shooting a dart into their heart. Even though you apologize later, the dart has left a wound. Shoot enough darts and soon there is no more room for love because the heart is full of wounds. Be careful of what you say in anger.

Don't forget your life experiences. Remember what it was like to be a new employee or new to the neighborhood and trying to figure out where everything is. Remember what it was like to be poor or less fortunate and working hard to make a living. Remember what it was like to be a child, filled with wonder and curiosity for the world around you yet vulnerable to the big people in your life. When you encounter people in those situations as you go through life, soften your interaction with the memory of what it was like to be in that situation. Be compassionate and understanding of their uncertainty and confusion.

The only 100 percent surefire way to prevent pregnancy is by abstinence. There is no other form of birth control that will always work without fail short of sterilization; and even that has occasional failures.

Not all lessons in life are painless. Think about how you teach someone what "hot" is. How do you describe that? The only way to fully understand it is to get burned. There are lessons in life that have to be learned that way. Let your children get burned sometimes. It makes them more knowledgeable and informed.

Don't worry about the things you can't control. The world is a big and crazy place. While you can control what you do, you cannot control what all those other people out there are doing.

Some things will happen that you just can't stop. The best example of that is the weather. You might not want it to rain on the day you plan to picnic at the park but Mother Nature doesn't care. Don't fret about it. Just change the day you plan to go out or put on a raincoat and accept it.

Count your blessings, not your troubles. We all have troubles. Why do some people get through them better than others? We need to focus on the good things in our lives. There will always be problems. Accept it. Be glad for what you have. Know that you cannot appreciate the good things unless you have bad things to compare them to.

Have someone you can "bear all" to. Sometimes we get all balled up inside and can't seem to find a solution for our problems. Talking it out with someone can help you to clarify your thoughts and help you to put things in perspective. Don't be afraid to seek counseling.

Write letters when you can't bring yourself to talk about something. I was nearly dysfunctional by the time I was eighteen. I started seeing a psychologist but I was so tied up inside that I couldn't talk. I would come in for a session and just sit there, answering "yes" or "no" to the therapist's questions, unable to expand on any subject. I just couldn't bring myself to talk even though I very much wanted help. After a few unsuccessful sessions, the doctor suggested that I write my thoughts and feelings down during the week and bring them when I next came in. So I did. I sat while he read the papers, answering questions as he went through my notes. Slowly, I was able to open up and eventually went on to have productive therapy sessions. I credit him with saving my life and helping me to achieve a meaningful and fulfilling existence. He never gave up on me where someone else might have dismissed me because we couldn't establish a relationship.

Everyone has good in them. You might get taken by an unscrupulous crook, but why cheat yourself out of good relationships on the fear that one no-good person will take advantage of you? People usually act the way you expect them to act.

Never underestimate the power you have on others. One year, I taught a statistics course during a very hot summer season. There was no air-conditioning in the building. The class was three hours a night for four nights a week for six weeks. It was brutal. Thirty-one students started the class. Only seventeen finished. On a lark, I got some rocks and wrote "I survived BUS301" on each rock along with one or two statistical formulas. On the last day of class, I handed them out to my students, congratulating them on a very difficult achievement and "rewarding" each one with a rock, telling them they could do anything they put their minds to.

A couple of years later, a woman came up to me in the store where I was shopping. She said she had been a student in that summer statistics class. Sometime after that class, she had been going through a divorce at the same time she lost her job and her child was seriously ill. She had contemplated suicide because her troubles seemed overwhelming. While she was packing up her household goods, she came across the rock. Looking at that rock brought a smile to her face. She told herself that if she could survive that statistics class, she could survive anything. Shortly thereafter, she found a job and soon had her life back on track. She thanked me profusely for saving her life. What did I know? I was just giving out rocks.

Money doesn't solve anything; it just creates new problems. The only difference between a rich person and a poor person is the amount of their bills. There was a follow-up study done of lottery winners to explore how their lives were changed after winning a million or more dollars. Most people were actually worse off than before they won. Organizations hounded them for donations to worthy causes. Relatives previously unknown showed up asking for money. Marriages broke up. Some people even committed murder to get the newfound money.

When I look at the rich and famous people in our society, I see their money hasn't protected them from life's vagaries. Their marriages often don't survive their success no matter how much money they have (examples include Jeff Bezos and Paul McCartney). Suicide rates are high (look at Kurt Cobain and Robin Williams). Their money doesn't protect them or their loved ones from death (examples include John Travolta and John Denver). Wealth doesn't protect them from drug abuse (see Michael Jackson and Whitney Houston). Rich people never know if someone is their friend because they like them or because they like their status and money. Who wants to live like that?

Blackmail only works if you keep the deed quiet. Fess up and the blackmailer no longer has power over you.

Never go shopping without a list. When you go shopping without a list, you wind up buying things you don't need and forgetting things you do need. Also, you might spend more than you wanted to by picking up those extra items. Likewise, apply this principle to all aspects of your life. Take a list of questions to an interview. Have a list of things to do for the day. Make up a list of topics to discuss with someone during an important conversation. There's nothing worse than saying, "I should have done that," or "I should have said this." Be prepared and you'll seldom find yourself regretting your actions.

People are never satisfied. I used to go to bingo games with my aunt. It was amusing to see people carry on about winning. If they won a game and had to share the prize, they wished they had won it alone. If they won the game alone, they wished they had won the full card. If they won the full card, they wished they had won the big jackpot. It never seemed to be enough. Rich people will always point to someone who is richer than they are.

It's all relative. I once met a woman who was quite overweight. During our conversation, she explained that everything in life is relative. She might look fat next to me, but she looked small next to a hippopotamus.

When I was eight years old, I met a young marine. He was tall and handsome in his dress uniform. I was awed and asked him how old he was. He told me he was eighteen. "Wow," I replied. "That's so old!" Today, an eighteen year-old person is quite young compared to me. Keep things in perspective.

Be aware of who's in politics. Understand what's going on in the world around you. The folks in politics form legislation that touches on our lives. They make laws that impact our homes, our education, our salaries, our taxes, every facet of our livelihood. Know who's in office and what they are doing.

Watch the news every day. Be aware of what's going on in the world. But don't obsess over what's happening. Today's news stations air twenty-four hours a day. They must fill the airwaves every minute of every day. As a result, they play images of horrible events over and over again. Talking heads endlessly debate the pros and cons of political issues.

Commentators drone on relentlessly about various topics. Tune in for the six o'clock news and turn it off at seven. Watch foreign news for a unique view of what's happening in America.

There are two primary motivators for human behavior–food and sex. Food for individual survival. Sex for survival of the species. We all watch those cute nature shows where all the females gather to give birth to their young and males engage in combat to see who will be the leader of the pack. Some breeds kill each other for the chance to mate. The drive for sex can be overwhelming.

I have seen men throw away their lives for sex–and not for a long-term, loving relationship but for a quick roll in the hay. I have seen men lose the love and respect of their family, give away their fortunes, and destroy their reputation and careers. One man even took his life after his affair was discovered. He knew it was wrong but he could not stop himself. I often wonder how the sex could have been worth his life. When a partner wails "But they didn't mean anything" after their infidelity has been discovered, they probably mean it. Men are especially plagued with the need to mate. No matter what a man looks like, he is interested in sex. His DNA demands it. And let's not forget that it takes two to tango. Women are also driven by a need to mate.

Let me add a caveat here, lest anyone think I am excusing bad behavior. Animals respond to a deep-seated need to propagate that drives their behavior. Human beings have the added ability to ponder their feelings. Coupled with willpower, although sometimes difficult, it is certainly possible to walk away from temptation.

The grass is always greener on the other side.

Talk to your children about sex before they start school. We are all exposed to so much in the media today. Televisions are everywhere–restaurants, bars, libraries, stores, schools, etc. Children see and hear about sex through exposure to these outlets. If you wait for that special time to have "the talk," you will be too late. Start discussions as early as age four or five years old.

Honesty is the best policy. You might get punished for something you did but it will be less painful than if you are caught lying about it. It is difficult to remember what you said to whom when you start trying to cover up your misdeeds. Tell the truth right away and get it over with.

There are rules about sex we must teach our children:
1. Do not touch a child. A person who tries to have sex with a child is called a pedophile. They put pedophiles in jail.
2. If someone says no, you must stop. Someone who tries to make someone have sex with them when that person does not want to is called a rapist. They put rapists in jail.
3. Respect other people's space. If they don't want to be touched, don't touch. That includes pats on the back, strokes on the arm, and hugs.
4. Don't talk about your sexual relationships with other people. Respect the privacy of the relationship.
5. Use a prophylactic to protect yourself against disease and prevent pregnancy. There are venereal diseases out there that will kill you.

Statistics. Mark Twain said "There are lies, damned lies, and statistics." I love numbers. They tell a story. I taught statistics for twenty-eight years. But you must be aware that statistics can be easily manipulated to say whatever you want. If someone quotes statistics to you, take it with a hefty piece of skepticism and ask yourself a few questions.

1. Who is giving you the information? If the informer has a personal interest in the issue, be wary. For example, if someone says 80 percent of the population favors gun ownership, it is possible the NRA (National Rifle Association) is reporting the numbers to support its position. Always ask yourself who is telling the story and what do they have to gain from it.

2. Who was surveyed? A survey can be skewed any way you want if you include a specific group of people amenable to your topic. For instance, gun advocates would do their survey in Texas where a great number of people approve of guns rather than in New York City where most people are against gun ownership.

3. How was the study conducted? Elements of a situation can be conveniently included or left out, depending on what the person wants the outcome to be. For instance: A study was done of sheep to determine if black sheep and white sheep eat the same amount of food (I know, the things they spend money on!). The published report declared that white sheep eat more than black sheep. When the study was reviewed, it turned out there are more white sheep than black sheep in the world. There had been no adjustment to account for the difference in the number of sheep. The study simply reported the raw

numbers. When the study was adjusted for the difference in numbers, it turned out that all sheep eat the same amount of food. Look at how the study was structured.

4.   What was included in the study? A report came out of a 1900s college that 67 percent of their female faculty was unmarried. It turned out that there were only three females on staff and two of them were single. The percentage sounded large but the actual numbers were very small.

Vote in every election. People suffered horrific experiences in trying to win the right to vote. Women, Blacks, Hispanics, Native Americans, Asians, and other groups all were victims of bigotry and prejudice in the formative years of the United States. They demonstrated, rioted, campaigned, and endured injuries and hardships. They did it for themselves and they did it for you. Exercise your right to vote in every election. It is a hard won privilege.

You are ***the other guy***. When we look at things happening, we always imagine that it's going to happen to the other guy, not you. Well, guess what? There's a person somewhere out there who's thinking that something will happen to you because *you* are the other guy. Don't make the mistake of believing something won't happen to you just because you don't want it to.

Have a skill you can use aside from your regular job to make extra money when you need it. For instance, learn how to repair computers. Then you could work on your own nights and weekends fixing computers for friends and family. Or learn how to fix cars, mow lawns, sew clothes or any one of dozens of different skills that will allow you to make a little extra pocket change outside of your regular job.

It takes a man and woman to make a baby. When people want a child, it takes a man and a woman to create that life. And for those who respond that you can create life in a petri dish: it still requires an egg from a woman and sperm from a man. That's the law of nature and a fact of life.

If you can't say something nice, don't say anything at all. Keep your negative comments to yourself. The people around you might listen to your criticisms, but they will remember that you say unpleasant things about others. That means you probably say nasty things about them, too. If people's opinions matter to you, don't share your poor opinions of others with them.

Don't wait. When I first enlisted in the National Guard, there was a crusty old warrant officer who was getting ready to retire. He was excited about the new stage of his life. He and his wife were going to get an RV and explore the country. They had dreamed about it for years. He retired, sold his house, bought a motor home, and headed out. A month later, he returned, sold the motor home, and came by to visit. He told me not to wait until retirement to travel. By then, he discovered he and his wife were in poor health and not able to do the things they had planned to do. They couldn't take long hikes or climb hillsides or endure extended periods of physical exertion. He said, "Don't wait." We took that advice to heart and began camping and traveling as much as we could. As a result, we have been to all fifty states in America, several provinces in Canada, and even took a quick excursion into Mexico. If you have a dream, act on it as soon as you can. Don't wait.

Be sincere in your praise. Some people try to garner other's cooperation by complimenting them openly and heavily. They don't compliment because they really like the person but simply because they want something. That kind of praise is insincere. It causes most people to trust you even less because they can see through it. When you take the time to compliment someone, make sure you mean it and the praise is true.

Express gratitude daily. What a wonderful thing it is to wake every day and be alive! Many people will never reach your age or attain the things you have. Take a moment to thank God (or the Fates) for the good things in your life.

Pick your battles. Some people believe they have to be right all the time. It does not make you weak to concede a point now and then. Stand firm for the important issues and let the smaller ones go. Compromise is important to every relationship.

People are more likely to vocalize dissatisfaction than satisfaction. When you purchase a service or an item, say a meal in a restaurant or clothing in a store, you expect certain things. When it happens as you expect, then you don't say anything. After all, it's that person's job to satisfy the customer. If you are not happy with what happened, you are more likely to tell others how bad your experience was. Yet, when things go well, you have the opportunity to let everyone know as well. Be more open to complimenting people when they do what you expect. And *especially* when they do better than expected. You can even go a step further and compliment the company they work for. Spread the word when a vendor hires good people.

Thank your spouse/significant other and children for something they do every day. Even for something as simple as helping with a chore, doing homework, or preparing a meal. Everything someone does in the family is a gift. They could refuse to do those things. Thank them for doing them.

The shortest distance between two points is a straight line.

Praise in public and criticize in private. Everyone wants to be admired. When you praise a coworker or fellow volunteer in public, you help them attain respect. Save your criticism for a private, one-on-one conversation behind closed doors. If you criticize someone in public (and that includes your children), you embarrass them. Furthermore, they will resent you for making them look bad in front of their peers. Some bosses think it will cause subordinates to perform better. It will only cause hard feelings and leave that boss vulnerable to retribution.

When presented with a difficult choice, make a list of pros and cons. I often told my children to draw up a chart when faced with a hard decision. List the choices at the top of the page. Down the side of the chart, make a list of all the things under consideration. Assign a value from 1 to 5, with 1 being the lowest and 5 being the highest. For each choice, enter a value. Total each column. The one with the highest value should be the one you choose. If the choice that has the highest value to you does not make you happy, then maybe you really want the other choice. Review the values you assigned. In the end, go with the choice that results in the highest value.

For example, say you are considering taking a new job. Label two columns at the top of the page, one column for the new job and one for your present job. Down the left hand side of the page, list the aspects that are important to you; e.g., salary, location, responsibilities, benefits, etc. Assign each aspect a value from 1 to 5, with 1 being the least valuable and 5 being the most valuable. Then total each column and select the one with the highest value. If they come out the same, then you'll just have to flip a coin.

Compare yourself to someone less well off than you. Most people compare themselves to someone who is better off than they are. This only serves to depress you and make you feel deprived. When you compare yourself to someone less well off, you realize how good you have it. Going to a new doctor always does this for me. They give you multiple pages listing dozens of medical maladies and ask you to check off what you have. There are so many conditions and illnesses listed on those sheets of paper I don't have that I realize how well I actually am.

Hindsight is 20/20. It's often difficult to see the full picture when you are deep in the middle of an event. After it's over, it's easier to look back and see what actions were in play. In evaluating a situation, keep in mind that not all facts were known at the time an event took place.

Read biographies. It is amazing to discover that a millionaire or famous person was once disliked or suicidal or homeless. We look at successful people and think they have always had it easy. In many cases, it was the adversity they suffered that made them strong enough to overcome obstacles to their success. I find biographies inspirational. You are not alone in your struggles. Reading of other people's difficulties can inspire you to conquer your own problems. Abraham Lincoln lost sixteen elections before being elected president of the United States. Harland Sanders was fired from several jobs and had failed businesses before Kentucky Fried Chicken made him famous. Mike Lindell was a down-and-out drug addict on the verge of self-destruction when he created My Pillow.

Birds can't smell. Well, all except the vulture. If you find a baby bird that has fallen out of the nest, put it back. The old wife's tale that says the mama bird can smell that humans touched her baby is not true.

Always use a ground guide. This comes from our RV activity but extends to everything we do that we are unsure of. Use a guide (i.e., mentor) to help you get through something you have to do. Don't be afraid to ask for help when you need it. Take the opportunity to learn from someone who knows more than you do.

Always use your manners. Saying "please" or "thank you" or "excuse me" is an example of good manners. When you express them, especially to those closest to you, you show respect for that person. Even though my husband and I have been married for fifty years, we still excuse ourselves when we fart or belch. We thank each other for bringing something that we asked for, or washing the dishes, or holding the door open, or for countless other courtesies. These little gestures make others feel appreciated.

Find a Hero to Admire. Heroes can be such an inspiration. They can be famous people, fictional characters, or real folks. I admire George Washington, Abraham Lincoln, Spock (from Star Trek), my husband's aunt, and my mother. When I remember their character traits and try to copy them in my own life, they help to make me a better person.

***Learn the difference between what you want and what you
need***. We need food. A hamburger will work just as well as a
sirloin steak. A thirty-dollar shirt will cover your back just as
well as a three-hundred-dollar shirt. We need shelter, clothes,
water, food, and heat in the winter. All the other stuff is
extraneous and not essential to your life. Don't waste your
life chasing nonessential things.

The best relationships are long term. When we had been
married around thirty-five years, we got a dog from the
animal shelter. We talked about a name for her. I wanted
something that started with a *B*, like Boomer or Bear, but
more feminine. We threw a few names around and decided to
think about it for a while. I went in to take a shower and
while in there, I thought of the name Bonnie. After the
shower, I walked back into the den to tell my husband about
the name I thought of. Before I could utter a word, he blurted
out that he thought Bonnie would be a good name. I found it
amazing that we had both decided on exactly the same name.
It seemed we had developed some kind of psychic link over
the years.

I then began to pay attention to the times we had the
same ideas and it turned out to be quite often. While driving
in the car, I would think *That's a really nice color for that
house*. I'd turn to Paul and before a word got out of my
mouth, he would say, "That's a really nice color for that
house." He would repeat my thought word for word. It was
uncanny!

When he'd go out to run an errand, I would send him thoughts like *Pick up a pizza for dinner* or *Buy bread and milk*. About 90 percent of the time, he got the message. Or he would come home and say, "Guess who I saw at the store?" or "I ran into what's-his-name today." I would then name the person. Despite the fact that we know hundreds of people–me from teaching college classes, traveling with the Army, or serving in church or him with his handyman business–we almost always know who the other one is talking about. It is both fun and amazing that we can think so much alike. This is a very enjoyable and amusing part of our relationship.

Hope for the best but plan for the worst.

If you are unsure about an action you are thinking about taking, ask yourself three questions: Is it unethical? Is it immoral? Is it illegal? If you can answer no to all three questions, then finish off with imagining that your action is broadcast on the 6:00 p.m. news as a major breaking story. Would you be embarrassed to have your friends and family see it? If you couldn't face your spouse, parents, children, coworkers, or best friend because of what you are considering, then it probably is not a good action to take.

Know your family story. When we were young, we didn't care much for family ties. When we got married, my husband wouldn't tell his mother where we were going to live so she couldn't interfere in our lives. Thank goodness, we got over ourselves!

My mother called one day to say that a cousin from Holland was visiting and asked me to come meet her. I was busy and wasn't really interested in meeting someone from so far away who (I thought) I wouldn't see again. Later in life, I developed an interest in genealogy and discovered a whole family line I knew nothing about. I wish I had taken the time to meet that cousin and perhaps kept in touch. Today I have the resources to travel overseas. Wouldn't it be nice if I could travel to Holland and meet those relatives?

When our son was born, we wanted to look at baby pictures in order to see who the baby looked like. Our parents had baby pictures of us and we were eager to look them over. Suddenly, family was important to us. Isn't it funny how things turn out? My husband's mother suddenly went from being "your mother" to "my mother-in-law." We became family in a new way.

Everyone likes to laugh. It feels good. Think about the people you like to be around. It's usually the cut-up in the crowd; the person who always makes everyone laugh.

People are quicker to excuse themselves for misbehavior than they are other people who do the same thing. When Monica Lewinsky was testifying before Congress about her relationship with President Bill Clinton, a friend of mine told me that he watched the proceedings from his bed where he lay next to his mistress. He was very critical of the president's infidelity while he carried on his own extramarital affair with impunity. People find it easy to excuse themselves when they do something wrong yet hold others to a higher standard.

Don't be afraid to apologize. I took a job at Macy's Department Store one Christmas season because I needed some extra money for the holidays. I was assigned to a department that sold picture frames and other knick knacks. As it got closer to Christmas, the lines at my register got longer and longer. By the time people got to the register, they were pretty cranky. Some had waited half an hour or more. Their arms were tired from holding their purchases, their feet hurt from standing for so long, and they were hot (it was winter in New York and everyone was wearing coats and scarves). One day, I apologized to a customer for the long wait. She perked right up and reassured me it wasn't my fault. Then she proceeded to have a pleasant chat with me while I rang up her purchases. From then on, I began to apologize for the long wait to each customer as they came up to the register. Almost every customer became a nice person who fully understood that the lines were long because it was that time of year. The transformation of the mood of everyone was amazing. Even though it wasn't my fault that the lines were so long, my acknowledgment of their discomfort somehow made their experience less uncomfortable. They learned that someone from the store understood the aggravation they had gone through to buy something there.

We are all products of our life experiences. The way we react to situations depends on what we have experienced in our lives. When I was stationed in Iraq in 2005, there were mortar attacks on American military facilities. Some sites had many more attacks than others. Every base had concrete structures that you could stand under when an attack happened. We experienced very few attacks on Camp Freedom in Bagdad and our structures basically stood unused. A young lieutenant transferred in from a forward base dubbed Camp Mortaritaville (soldiers can make jokes about anything). That base suffered daily mortar attacks and he was very hypersensitive. We were walking around the base when a bomb exploded in the ordnance yard. Thinking the base was under attack, he immediately jumped under a concrete bunker for protection. It turned out to be only the ordnance detail blowing up confiscated explosives. We laughed at the lieutenant for his reaction. His experience had taught him to seek shelter at the sound of explosives where our experience had taught us to ignore them.

Don't feed ducks bread. Bread causes a metabolic deficiency in the wings of ducks. If they eat too much bread during their developing years, it will cause a condition known as angel wing where their wings will deform and grow in a swept back condition. They will not be able to fly or even flap their wings. It is a cruel and life threatening condition for a duck. Nature provides for the wildlife. Leave them to eat what's natural to them and keep the people food at home.

Accept responsibility for the things you do, even when it's not your fault. When my son was two years old, we stopped at an old-fashioned general store to do some shopping. He picked up a bag of candy to buy. I let him hold on to it while we walked around the store. Suddenly, the bag burst open and candies spilled out all over the floor. It wasn't his fault. The seam on the bag had just let go. I explained to him that although he did not directly cause the bag to break with his little two-year old hands, he did cause the mess and had to help clean up. Such is life. We get involved in things that happen even though we didn't cause them. If you are in such a situation, cheerfully pitch in and clean up the mess that results.

Don't drop an animal off in the "wilderness" if you no longer want it or can't keep it. The ability to hunt, to find shelter, to recognize and escape predators are all skills taught by a parent. If you have been feeding your animal kibble for the entire time you have had it, that's all it knows. There is no wild instinct that will instantly enable your pet to survive on its own. Think about what would have happened to you if your parents had dropped you off in the woods (there are some parents who have fantasized about this, I'm sure). Would you have known which berries were all right to eat and which weren't? How to shelter from the elements? How to escape a bear or wolf? If you cannot or do not want to keep an animal any more, for whatever reason, bring it to a shelter. Give your pet a chance at survival.

You can chase critters away yourself. If a raccoon or squirrel takes up residence in your attic, you can chase it away yourself. Simply put on a bright light and have a radio tuned to a news station broadcasting all the time. Put rags soaked in ammonia in the middle of the room. Animals like it dark and quiet. Take that away and they'll look for another place to live. If you call a specialist in pest removal, there is a good chance that you are consigning the animal to death. Once the wildlife is gone, cover up the hole they got in through.

Give gifts if you want gifts. My grown child once complained to me that no one gave him gifts for his birthday. I asked who he gave gifts to. When he replied that he didn't give any, I asked him why he should expect anyone to give him a gift. People will usually reciprocate when they are given a gift. Folks start out receiving gifts as young children but as they grow older, they are expected to return the effort. If they don't, the gifts usually stop coming.

A gift belongs to the person who receives it. Once you give a gift to someone, it's theirs to do with as they want. You no longer have any say about it. If they want to give it away, throw it away, store it away, whatever–it's theirs. If you tie strings to it, then you haven't really given anything away. You've attached controls.

Use self-deprecating humor. It seems there is always someone, somewhere who will take offense at a joke whether it's ethnic, cultural, religious, or sexual. Making fun of yourself is the only sure way to stay out of the radar of the "offended people."

When someone gives you something, say thank you. No one HAS to give you anything. Not for your birthday. Not for your anniversary. Not for your graduation. Not for anything. When someone takes the time to give you something, they have invested effort in doing it. They thought about the occasion, looked for the gift, wrapped it, and presented it. Show appreciation for the gesture by thanking the person for the gift. Even if you don't like it.

Children model their parent's behavior. I witnessed a grown woman of three small children fly into a violent rage because she was angry at her husband. Her mother and I were visiting in her home at the time. She stomped down the hall, spewing invectives about her spouse and throwing things around the house. Her mother tried to calm her down but she shoved her out of the way as she ranted and raved. Her children seemed to melt away into the background while she carried on. Apparently, they had seen that kind of behavior before.

The next day, at a Little League game during which her son had a meltdown, the same woman commented that he "has to learn to control himself." Why should he? He has a role model right there in his own home. He will act as he has witnessed his parents act.

Americans have lots of disposable income today. In 1960, families had one car and one TV in the house. People had two pairs of shoes; one pair for dress up and one pair for everyday wear. If you wanted a new toy or item of clothing years ago, you hoped to get it for your birthday or Christmas. No one made extraneous purchases except for special occasions. Today, it seems everyone old enough to drive owns a car. Homes now have four or more TVs–one in each bedroom, one in the den/living room, and even one in the kitchen/dining room. We went on a cruise where a friend of ours brought three suitcases; two for her clothes and one for her shoes. Americans have so much disposable income that they now hire people to hold their stuff for them. Storage companies have popped up all across the country for the express purpose of storing stuff.

Continue seeking training/education in your field throughout your career. I was working as the manager of an off-airport parking lot. A man applied for a job as a van driver. When I looked at his application, I saw he had a PhD in computer science. I asked him why he would want a minimum-wage job with his qualifications. He explained that he had worked for the same company for many years. When they went out of business, he found the computer world had changed and his skills were no longer relevant. Had he kept up with the changes in the technology that affected him, he would not have found himself on the street with outdated skills.

When on a crowded bus or train or plane or in a crowded airport or bus terminal, do not put your bag on the seat next to you. Put it on the floor between your feet and give someone else a chance to sit down, just like you.

A skilled captain is not forged on calm seas.

Always offer your seat to an older or disabled person when on public transportation. A mother with babies would also appreciate a seat.

Beware of the Internet. There are no controls on what is posted on the Internet. No one oversees who is posting or how long something remains online. It was discovered that a teenager was posting a blog giving medical advice as though he were a doctor. Take anything you read on the Internet with a hefty dose of skepticism and always verify the information you glean.

Children will change your life forever. Nothing will ever be the same after you have a child. Your opinions will change. Your beliefs will change. Your relationships with family will change. You will be challenged in ways you never expected. You will make dozens of decisions about a host of life choices as the years go by. Do we give a weekly allowance or expect our youngster, as a member of the family, to help around the house without compensation? Should they do homework immediately upon coming home from school or play and do it after dinner? When do you start insisting they do chores?

What works for one child may not work for the next. Each child is a unique individual who responds to stimuli in various ways. How very challenging and, sometimes, frustrating.

Never use just one source for your information. Gather your information from several organizations. It is so easy to stay with one information source but no one is completely thorough or objective in reporting data. News articles are often colored with the reporter's perceptions. Historians relate the facts based on how they interpret them. If you want the full picture of an event, person, area, etc., use more than one source to inform yourself.

The Internet is forever. While working at Suffolk County Community College, fellow faculty members posted an item on the newly accessible Internet to see how long it would stay online. Years later, the item was still there.

Wikipedia is not a credible source. Anonymous volunteers provide information for Wikipedia. While its purpose is commendable (to provide an online free content encyclopedia for everyone to share knowledge), it should only be used as a "kick-off" to any research project you are contemplating. Go to authoritative sources to collect your facts.

Criticize a plan only when you have a better alternative to offer. Complaining for the sake of complaining does no one any good. You don't know all the nuances of a leader's situation–all the information that person knows–the restrictions, the concessions, the requirements, etc. If you are part of a project/operation, only speak up if you think you have a better alternative to offer. Otherwise, keep quiet. Just because you don't like the plan doesn't mean you have a right to complain about it. The plan, as flawed as it is, is the best anyone can come up with.

The only constant in life is change. No matter how good, or bad, things are right now, your situation will change. Nothing remains the same forever.

Fifty to 100 percent of communication is nonverbal. Have you ever watched an old married couple at a buffet line or church potluck? The husband strolls down the tables, looking over the array of food before him. Suddenly, he spots a dish he likes. He plucks up a tasty morsel and starts to bring it to his mouth. Halfway up, he looks over and sees his wife staring at him: direct steely gaze, lips firmly pressed together, arms crossed, back rigid. He freezes as they lock eyes. You can imagine the communication between them goes something like: "Now, John. You know what Dr. Jones said. You have to watch your diet and *that* is not allowed." There's a quick flash of momentary defiance then, crestfallen, he slowly puts the item back. A whole conversation passed between them and no one said a word.

Have you ever spoken with someone and just knew they were lying to you? You are most likely picking up on their body language on a subconscious level. We convey information in so many different ways: crossed arms and legs tell if you are relaxed or tense, the direction your eyes look when recounting a story say that you are either remembering facts or making something up, how close or far you stand from someone indicates how comfortable you are with them. Most communication, however, comes from the face: a smile, a frown, a smirk, a raised eyebrow, a wink, slitted eyes, bared teeth, laughter, wrinkled brow, etc. It all speaks a silent language.

And there are many different cultural variations. Be careful when addressing someone from another country. Their body language can be very confusing.

Take the year after graduation to work. Very often, when you graduate from high school, you don't know what you want to do. Your whole life stretches out before you and seems overwhelming. All students should take a year to go work somewhere or travel, then go to college or skills-training school. It will give them a better appreciation for the need for further education or training and provide a more well-rounded understanding of the working world.

College is not for everyone. This may sound like an odd thing for an educator to say, but I watched young men and women travel through my classroom for twenty-eight years. Some were there to learn something and some were there simply because their parents told them to go to college. They didn't want to be there. They didn't really know what they wanted. They almost always failed. In fact, 70 percent of first-time-to-college students drop out. About half of those will return to college later. There are well-paying blue-collar jobs that don't require college. If your children don't want to go to college, allow them to learn other skills.

Believe in a higher power. I've seen enough unusual things in my lifetime to believe there is more than this mortal life. I have been hugged by a ghost, saved from disasters, and received quiet direction.

I was sent to Iraq in 2005. My job was to lead a team of eight people in tracking down Army Reserve equipment left in theater. I split the eight members into two teams: one team of three in Iraq and four team members in Kuwait with me traveling between locations. A problem arose between the team leader and non-commissioned officer (NCO) in Iraq. My sergeant major said he would fly to Iraq to resolve the issue but the next day decided not to go. I then decided to go, but it took a couple of days to get a flight.

When I arrived in Iraq, I found the NCO very distraught. Her domestic partner back home had just terminated their relationship. She was very upset and looking for someone to talk to. We walked to an outside seating area near a food truck and sat down to talk. There was a sandstorm in the area and the air was thick with dust. After about a half hour, when the NCO was done talking and all cried out, we continued to sit for a while. I don't know why. We just stayed in place.

Suddenly, I noticed a soldier, another NCO, pacing back and forth behind the food truck. He was agitated and working himself into quite a state. One of the Iraqi civilians working on post was running back and forth between a truck and a building. He appeared to be terrified. Then the NCO's helmet came rolling by and I realized something was very wrong. Knowing that NCOs respond better to NCOs than officers, I sent my soldier to see what was going on. My soldier informed me that the NCO's unit had been attacked last week while on patrol, and two members of their squad had been killed during a firefight. Today, he was assigned Hadji duty. This was considered little more than a baby-sitting assignment. Locals were brought on base to perform maintenance-and-repair functions and soldiers were assigned to supervise them. The NCO was very upset with Iraqis, blaming the citizenry for his friend's deaths, and was whipping himself into a rage. It was clear that he was going to explode and possibly kill the group of six locals he was supervising. My soldier was able to talk him down and restore calm and order.

What was remarkable about this situation was the timing of the whole event. My sergeant major was supposed to have arrived there four days earlier. He changed his mind and it took me a couple of days to get to the base. We came walking out in a sandstorm when we normally would have stayed inside. After we were done talking, we continued to stay in place. There is no doubt in my mind that the entire situation was orchestrated by a higher power. Because I was there at the exact time and place that murder was about to happen, I had a hand in stopping it. A guardian angel was hard at work.

You are a unique, unrepeatable miracle of God. Each person is a gift to the world. Don't be ashamed of who or what you are. You are a product of your parent's actions, who are a product of their parent's actions, who are a product of their parent's actions, and so on and so on. You are a certain ethnicity and gender because that was the straw you drew in the lottery of life. Don't resent it or fight it. Learn to accept and embrace your individuality. You are who you are. That makes you a character. And characters are what make life so interesting.

Everyone dies. Some of us live to a ripe old age. Others die sooner because of disease, illness, accident, or violence. Be prepared. Have a will completed that ensures your final wishes will be carried out. Have a life insurance policy that covers your funeral expenses. If you can afford it, purchase a life insurance policy that leaves enough money for your family to live on for at least one year or more after your departure.

Be of service to others. Some of my happiest moments were when I was in service to others. I felt joy when selling poppies at the street fair for the American Legion. I experienced comradery in helping to set up for a yard sale or Christmas fair at our local church. I felt pride when I taught boys and girls scouting skills. I was filled with wonder when I released a bird I helped to raise at a wildlife rescue center. There is fulfillment and satisfaction in striving to make the world a better place. Find a way to be of service to others. You will find great satisfaction in helping others.

I hope you enjoyed this compendium of witticisms and lifetime observations. Remember, life is an adventure. The people and places that share the world with us are so very interesting. Enjoy the journey.